RUBIK'S CUBE

A LONG FORGOTTEN COLLECTION OF POEMS FROM CHILDHOOD AND ADOLESCENCE

NISHA SANU

Copyright © Nisha Sanu
All Rights Reserved.

ISBN 978-1-68509-246-7

This book has been published with all efforts taken to make the material error-free after the consent of the author. However, the author and the publisher do not assume and hereby disclaim any liability to any party for any loss, damage, or disruption caused by errors or omissions, whether such errors or omissions result from negligence, accident, or any other cause.

While every effort has been made to avoid any mistake or omission, this publication is being sold on the condition and understanding that neither the author nor the publishers or printers would be liable in any manner to any person by reason of any mistake or omission in this publication or for any action taken or omitted to be taken or advice rendered or accepted on the basis of this work. For any defect in printing or binding the publishers will be liable only to replace the defective copy by another copy of this work then available.

Dear Circumstances,

This book is dedicated to you.

Contents

Disclaimer	*vii*
Preface	*ix*
Acknowledgements	*xi*

RUBIK'S CUBE

1. Vision	3
2. Relationships	4
3. Sense	5
4. Present	6
5. Loss	7
6. Curtain	8
7. Desire	9
8. Wake	10

And Some Others

9. The Cup	13
10. A Game Of Chess	14
11. Rights	15
12. For Sale	16
13. Life's Last	17
14. The Poisonous Fangs	18
15. When Night Comes…	19
16. This Little Dream	20
17. Not True? Or Not?	21
18. A Moth	22
19. A Painted Hull	23

Contents

20. A Sunset…and A Little Less	24
21. One Painful Night	25
22. War Of The Soul	26
23. (untitled: Dated 22.01.2006)	28
24. A Moment To Forget	29
25. Unbound	30
26. I Stood Draped In Black	31
27. I Was A Writer	34
Life Isn't Too Short	37

Disclaimer

This is a work of fiction. Names, characters, places, and incidents either are the products of the author's imagination or are used fictitiously. Any resemblance to actual persons, living or dead, businesses, companies, events, or locales is entirely coincidental.

Preface

Writing is for the recluse, as many believe. Though I do not believe it to be applicable for all, in my case, it is deceptively true. Deceptively because many do not believe me to be a recluse, true because many know I'm one. If given my way, I'd hole up in my own world and never come out. But it's been some time since I've given up my haunt and walked out in the open to love and life.

Most of the poems in here were written between the period of 2004 and 2012. Sparing a few, they are simple thoughts that I chose to keep over the years. Looking back as an adult, I discarded a few, and kept some that I feel should have been discarded, only because they traces of a quiet childhood I've left behind.

The first section consists of incomplete thoughts and stories pruned to a few lines, sometimes as little as two. They leave a lot unsaid, yet cry out the turmoil of the mind.

The second section are mostly old poems that I chose to store. They are again, random thoughts that left a trail of words on the tip of my pen.

They are nothing, yet everything to me.

Acknowledgements

Writing has always been my identity. It is, and always has been me. For this, I thank my parents. They have not only encouraged me to write but have been proud of it as well. This was the first stepping stone to my confidence in my words.

Thank you, Sanu, for always pushing me to publish my book despite my resistance. You've taken me to publishers and constantly reminded me that my writings aren't mine alone; they belong to the world. This is what a writer, or rather, a poet needs.

Thank you, Dr.Vijay Nair, for being one of the best mentors I've had during my college days, though I know I've never been able to live up to your expectations, drifting too far away soon after.

Thank you, Winnie, Reethu, Anju, Dhanusha, Nimmy, Jomily, and Jay for being my strongest support through all my trials. You all stood by me through every struggle and all my successes. That is true friendship.

Thanks to all my teachers throughout my academic life for teaching me the true value of discipline and respect.

A huge thanks to all my friends who have supported and criticized me. You all have helped me gain perspective in life.

Thank you, Vishnu, for being the brother you are. You are the one I lay the hope of my old age on.

Thank you Aaditya, Prithvi, and Ima, my kids, for showing me the joys of a life I was so skeptical about.

ACKNOWLEDGEMENTS

Thanks to everyone who has and hasn't been a part of my life. I have the whole world to thank, for without it, I wouldn't be able to do what I love doing - write!

RUBIK'S CUBE

1. Vision

The picture
does not end
With the
Wooden frame.

****

                                        Our walls have b'come tall,
                                              Our vision short,
                                                     We think high,
                                                           See less.

****

2. Relationships

"He fell a hundred storeys to his death,
but not before he broke his heart with her last breath."

****

> You smile at the thunder
> breaking atop the hill,
> While the sand slowly seeps
> through your clenched fists,
> Knowing, in vain, you have tried
> To build castles in the air,
> In vain, you have tried
> To keep him close.

****

3. Sense

Bearing Nothing
In Nothingness
Is nothing compared to
Nothingness in Nothing.

****

> Escapism
> is kicking the goat
> That
> chewed your food

4. Present

The sound
of the first clod of earth
Makes you feel the 'Past Tense'
In its realest sense.

****

Just this night
to slight
The only dream
I had.

5. Loss

The cut the vein of the scorned green leaf
And abandon it at twilight
Then to scream at the injustice
Of the dark dark night!!

                ****

                If memories could be burnt
                And sent down the sacred Ganges
                I wonder
                If we would finally be happy,
                Or would we still run like madmen
                In search of those blessed, lost, cinders…?..

6. Curtain

Sometimes just a tear says it all,
And another one ends it all.

****

I wonder
At the Present. Is it there?
The abundance of non-existence?

7. Desire

If there's nectar left still,
In your heaving bosom,
Save some, darling,
For the journey cumbersome,
In the fiery, that'll suck the water dry,
Till the day your last blessed drop,
Spills the wounded images
Of recklessness
That killed the future
And tortured the past..

****

The pinching pain
Of those moments you thought
were yours
But never were
But still you smiled
To save the pain
To save the faces.

****

8. Wake

I plucked the rose for my lady love
So that she could give it, sans thorns,
To the man of her dreams..
             ****

                              It dawned on my broken heart
                                        That even the brook
                                            Was a deadly swim
                                                    To you.

             ****

And some others

...dusted off the shelf...

9. The Cup

The cup fell off the lip
And broke int' two
Though I glued it to be as good as new
Cracks remained, a few.

10. A Game of Chess

A king, or queen,
a soldier, horse, a rook,
or an elephant,
Is what a game of chess is about?
A step ahead, or a step aside,
A sword, a fall, or a kill!
A sense of triumph or a final loss
A game, merely one, but isn't that what
Is life about?

11. Rights

The vintage-worn
Rusted keys
Burdened
Upon the shoulders
Of the hunchback,
Guarding
The ancestral home
With a knowing smile
That nerve-wrecking
Silence,
Only so long
As the hand falls
Upon the ripe mango
Fallen
Among the stale ones.

12. For Sale

So she put
a spoonful
Of memories
In a bowl
coated
In antiquity
And fragility
And
sold them
for free
Before embracing
The wide
and
Endless waters.

13. Life's Last

Every breath will seem priceless
When your time here is less,
Every moment gone, you wish
to drag back and relish.
But there's nothing for you left
Only your beloved pained and bereft,
Till the life's greatest truth comes to fetch
you from the doors of inevitable death.

14. The Poisonous Fangs

The poisonous fangs of seduction takes me down
To the untold depths of nothingness,
Where the stakes are high, life a senseless drumbeat,
Breathing brazen, the primitive soul taking a plunge
Defacing the man, adorning the shroud
When all the world feels deserving, for lying, and impersonating
the imagined colours of civilization.

15. When night comes…

The night skies await
To smother
The hypocritical veins
Afloat
On the majestic chamber
Of dysfunction
And sly
religious quotient,
With revered ignorance
Of the bloodstained axe
In the skeletal hands
Of a smiling
Grim reaper!!
****

Don't bother
It's just 'round the corner!!
****

16. This Little Dream

Let me transcend all Time
To break new waves upon your shore
And light the eternal flame
Of love.
Wherein let me reign
As the queen, yet your princess
And at nights in passion
As your thirst.
Love me beyond reason
And tell me this life is meaning-
less. Tell me
It all begins in you, and ends there too.
Give me your dreams, to see,
So I may live in my grave
And breathe,
In unreality
Of how much you love me.

17. Not True? Or Not?

I'm learning to 'accept the reality,'
The so-called one they say will happen anyway.
'Discard your emotions. Its no use,
The faster you accept, the lesser your hurt'
No use. Yes. No use.
No use, but it hurts me still- on the road
At my home, among the trees, at work.
It hurts me still, the reality.
It hurt before, when I dreaded it,
It hurts now, still.
It may be the poor writer's deluded mind
Failing to meet that'll anyway come,
Or maybe the delinquent who missed-
a few crucial lessons
In what they call 'practicality.'
And it's there, the hurt
Real.
It's real, the reality-and so is the hurt.
As always, this one again,
Alone will I have to face
Among the proponents of *******!!

18. A Moth

A little moth
Breaking its flight
In the clasps of fate,
fighting, unfearing
the end.

19. A Painted Hull

A painted hull
On a weathered rock
Memories
Prayful lips
Little imprints on the bottom
And fading paint
Only
Till the mites are no more
Or the hull.

20. A Sunset…And a Little Less

A sunset that sprinkled thoughts
Of waves that never were; of lives
held in turmoil over the years
Of pain that never ceased, and help
that never came.
A sunset that cared a little less, for
the wails of the shore, a little pine,
and a little tear, that never told
the story
of its exile from youth.
A sunset that shouted rebellion,
Killed traditions and broke the laws.
A sunset that danced drunk
from the goblet of time
and relentless age
running to quench its bloodthirst.
And
a sunset that never set
over the hills, in hope
to sprinkle seeds
of ageless time
and timeless age.

21. One Painful Night

One painful night of sleeplessness
Wondering what came knocking at the door,
Death, Disease, Common Cold
Or merely some old weary traveler,
Till the hooded shadow finally stood
And stared,
Why, perhaps I'd never know,
Contemplating the freshness of the unwilling meat?
And I, in an endless terrifying glance
stood up to gulp down my fearfulness
Until the morning sun rose to drive
The unwelcome guest
Out of the wretched door.

22. War of the Soul

If Karna himself, the son of Sun,
Was ground beneath the Pandava ego,
If Sita herself, the manifestation of chastity,
Was fed to the ultimate test of Agni,
Can we, the fossilized dreams of mankind,
Ever hope to shelter our children,
from the gunmen of betrayal, mass murder?
Can we ever give, the unbroken promise
Of life? When life itself is *Maya*?
We, brought up but believing the Illusion in Truth
and Truth in Illusion. Forever in search of the lost meaning
among the countless folds of the Present. Momentarily
when Present races behind our clutches in dizzying speeds.
When we stand in wonder at the truth of Present itself, and try
to hold in vain the unconquerable Master of Space and Time,
Desperate for once, to prove wrong, the legends and traditions
ensconced in the watertight culture of mankind.
The eternal struggle, the war with Time. For what?
To displace Truth? The inevitable? If meaning itself is meaningless,
Where does the Mother build nest for her nestlings?
Where does Man build his moment of Glory?

If this be not the war with the Gods, then do we fight with us?

Is this the war of the inner souls, hidden within its own turmoils,

killing one another, till Reason leaves the Body behind?

23. (Untitled: dated 22.01.2006)

Simply..
Simply because your sweetness
Stole my soul,
Simply because your songs
Swept away my sorrows,
Simply because your smile
Sent me spellbound,
Simply because your silence
Shared our stories,
Simply...
Simply because....

24. A Moment to Forget

You are my past
My broken dream,
You are the promise I failed
The words I battled
You are the smile I killed
The breath I smothered
You are...
You are the one I lost.

25. Unbound

Nevermore, more dangerous
The love of self-destruct
Binding the formless life
To the legacy of lies, and lies,
Surging through every vein of doom
Every moment, the blood
from the wounded body.
Yet she smiles, her score
unbeaten for evermore.

26. I Stood Draped in Black

I stood draped in black
Behind the lonesome pine, watching the pallbearers
laying the remnants of a life
While the rains pierced the deadly silence
Cutting through memories and stark reality
Of an absence for eternity.

The merciless sky battled on
Till I could watch no more, my shriveled body
being consumed by flames
After years of drunken dances, poisoned
By love
And unfaithfulness.
I walked away resigned, knowing
That from now, your hurt is greater than mine,
As you try to grapple in vain
at the irreversible, at the cracked leaves
You so carelessly once threw out the window
In mirth.

They all seem so distant now, the laughter
The throbbing hearts, the sweaty writhing bodies,

drugged by passion, blinded by love
The jingles as we hit the road, the clinking glasses
Fun. Frolic.
Fire.

Till the mermerizing hands pulled you away
From our endless walks, our silent talks
Leaving me frozen in time, my lips still playing
the dreams of Abba
Hurt, pained and burnt by loss
The time gone, forever.

For ages I watched the waters break onto the shore
As you came, left, came and left again,
Till the cracks could hold no more
The potion of love once so caringly poured
Into binding promises, now threadbare
From the rape of a countless vengeful moons.

That one last time you closed the door
Upon my smile, torn in agony,
I preyed upon my haven for the final
slip into mindlessness, not caring
Of your hurt, the kill,
Of the last consummation.
***

I still stare, at the breaking waters

Wondering now, why..

27. I Was A Writer

I was a writer
Of the glorious past
Till rudely awakened
To reality
bound in worldly pettiness
In a day's 'must do', 'coz u!'
It were my fantasy
Much much lesser than of real
Like being a writer wasn't much
but bedtime story, or
babies' building blocks.
Yet my Muses lonely
Pierced the unfed dreams
From desertion, deprivation
And of life's *little* glory.
With much trouble
I have yet to realize
That being a writer
Is my Calliope,
Most respectable of the Muses,
The highest pedestal.
My abandoned seedlings
will now satisfy

Within the fumes of 'encased reality'
For if breaking free
is being in chains,
Then why break free at all?

Life Isn't Too Short

Life isn't too short
But it is unpredictable
Chase your dreams
Fulfill your desires
Be content

Printed by Libri Plureos GmbH in Hamburg, Germany